A CONFLUENCE OF DREAMING

Tammy Ryan

BROADWAY PLAY PUBLISHING INC
New York
www.broadwayplaypublishing.com
info@broadwayplaypublishing.com

First printing: May 2012
Second printing: November 2013
I S B N: 978-0-88145-528-1

Book design: Marie Donovan
Page make-up: Adobe Indesign
Typeface: Palatino
Printed and bound in the U S A

ABOUT THE AUTHOR

Tammy Ryan's award winning plays have been performed across the United States and internationally. Plays include LOST BOY FOUND IN WHOLE FOODS, LINDSEY'S OYSTER, A CONFLUENCE OF DREAMING, DARK PART OF THE FOREST, BABY'S BLUES, F B I GIRL, THE MUSIC LESSON, and PIG. Her work has been developed at the New Harmony Project, Premiere Stages, Playwrights Theater of New Jersey and The Bonderman. Honors include the American Alliance of Theater and Education's Distinguished Play Award, the Pittsburgh Cultural Trust's Creative Achievement Award, a Heinz Creative Collaborative Grant and fellowships from Virginia Center for the Creative Arts and Pennsylvania Council of the Arts. An artist in residence with the Western Pennsylvania Young Writers Institute, Ryan also teaches playwriting at Point Park University. She is a member of the Dramatists Guild. For more information go to www.tammyryan.net.

A CONFLUENCE OF DREAMING received its first production at The Pittsburgh Playhouse by The Rep, the professional theater company of Point Park University (Ronald Allan-Lindblom, Artistic Producing Director) on 27 May 2010. The cast and creative contributors were:

CAROL..Bridget Connors
PETER/RESTAURANT OWNER......................Robert Turano
TED.. Sam Turich
MORGAN/WAITRESS..............................Connie Castanzo

Director..John Amplas
Scenic design..Steffi Mayer-Staley
Lighting design.........................Andrew David Ostrowski
Costume design............................... Michael Montgomery
Sound design... Steve Shapiro
Video design..Jessi Sedon
Stage manager... Alicia DeMara

CHARACTERS

CAROL, *48, wife and suburban "stay-at-home" mom, A K A*
COOLBREEZE *when she is online*

PETER, *49,* CAROL's *accountant husband A K A*
REGULARGUY

MORGAN, *17, their daughter about to start her senior year
in high school, idealistic, yet naïve*

TED, *early 30's, A K A* TALL+DARK+HANDSOME,
CAROL's *cybersex friend*

WAITRESS, *played by actress playing* MORGAN

RESTAURANT OWNER, *played by actor playing* PETER

SETTING

ACT ONE *takes place in* CAROL *and* PETER's *suburban Pittsburgh home. Specifically in the "great room" which used to be their kitchen living room and entry way, currently under various stages of construction as the play progresses.*

ACT TWO *takes place in a Thai restaurant in New York City, in* TED's *studio apartment on the Lower East Side, and once again, in Pittsburgh.*

Both acts also take place in "cyber space." Minimal, flexible set, is best. Any blackouts should be brief.

Time: summer of 2001: late July through September 10, 2001. The last scene takes place on the night before September 11th

Note: In establishing the convention of being online, I suggest keeping it simple. However you do that, whether with light, sound or staging or video/projection, the focus should be on the acting. Actors can begin "typing" but should eventually drop that and connect with who they are talking to. The important thing is that the cyberworld is established before realities merge, with characters crossing over from one to the other as necessary. Scene changes should be as fluid as possible.

ACT ONE

Scene One

(CAROL *alone*)

CAROL: In my dream I'm undressed, completely naked, exposed, except for a pair of red come get me shoes. There's no hiding in this room, which is great, empty and full of sunlight, just one bed on the floor. No blankets or sheets to crawl under, just a bare mattress. There is someone else in the room. I'm suddenly aware of the size of my ass, the cellulite on my thighs, and I'm trying to figure out which way to turn, to obscure, to flatter, but it's useless, there is no place. And then, I am overcome with this feeling that I am sexually attractive. I lie down on the bed and open my legs without shame, the red shoes float above my head like paragliding butterflies and I am immediately exotic and mysterious like an orchid from South America about to be seduced by the bee... And then I wake up and the dream disappears, immediately forgotten.

Scene Two

(*Evening. Pittsburgh, July 2001. Raining*)

(CAROL *and* PETER *are having dinner in their kitchen, which is in the midst of renovations.* PETER *is picking over his salad;* CAROL *lingers over her wine.*)

CAROL: So I told him if you're going to knock down that wall, you better be ready to clean it up at the end of the day because I can't live in a construction site. It's bad enough all this dust without climbing over mounds of mortar and bricks, I mean really Peter, he said he'd be done by the end of June two thousand and *one*. It's the end of July already and he's only just now working on that wall, at this rate he won't be done until September two thousand and *five*, I'm not exaggerating Peter, I think you better have a talk with him—

(PETER *starts choking on a peppercorn.*)

CAROL: I'm running around all day like a wild woman, working around this chaos, with no help from Morgan. Really Peter we gotta talk to her about pulling her weight around here because I'm reaching my limit, by the end of the day I drop into bed a stone—

(PETER *is still choking.*)

CAROL: Are you all right?

PETER: *(Nodding, still choking)* —Yes—

CAROL: Too much pepper in the vinagrette?

PETER: —no—

CAROL: I forget you don't like pepper.

PETER: —don't mind pepper.

CAROL: All my spices are in six different places because he still hasn't finished that built in for the spice rack. I don't get him, Peter, he starts one part of it then stops right before he finishes, it's like he has something against finishing. Do you want some water? The sink is working, at least, finally.

PETER: I'm fine.

CAROL: I'm going to do the Heimlick in a minute.

PETER: I'm fine.

CAROL: Okay. So how was dinner?

PETER: Fine.

CAROL: No pepper. But I think, it needed cumin,
of course, I couldn't find the cumin. You should be
grateful it's not our twentieth day of chinese. *(Pause)*
Nice to be alone, though. *(Beat)* Isn't it?

PETER: Uh? Oh, yeah. Of course. To being alone. *(Beat)*
When did Morgan say she'd be home?

CAROL: After eleven, she's closing tonight. And then
she said something about a meeting. Some political
thing, you better talk to her, Peter, she's got to get
those college applications in before September, or she's
going to be going to C C A C for godsake.

PETER: She's got another year of high school.

CAROL: I know, but she has to apply early for early
decision, there is so much competition now, why
doesn't anybody want to listen to me about this?

PETER: Let her have her summer. Don't you remember
the summer you were seventeen?

CAROL: She can have her summer as long as she writes
that essay, that's an important part of the application
and I can't write it for her.

PETER: All right I'll talk to her.

CAROL: The summer I was seventeen was a hundred
lifetimes ago. But of course, I remember it. *(She pours
the rest of the wine.)* OHHH, GOD. Why are we doing
this?

PETER: Because you wanted one great big room, so we
could all be linked by eye contact no matter what we
were doing.

CAROL: It's going to be the two of us staring at each other across the grand canyon. We should've done this ten years ago.

PETER: It'll still be nice.

CAROL: Don't you think it's strange?

PETER: What?

CAROL: That we're old enough to have a child going to college? It makes me want to turn back time.

PETER: It makes me want to win the lottery.

CAROL: You wait for them to get big and be independent so you can have your life back but then, when they finally do, you're old and gray—

PETER: Better than the alternative—

CAROL: When I was seventeen I never envisioned this. *(Suddenly remembering)* Omigod. Guess what I heard? John has cancer.

PETER: Oh my God.

CAROL: Colon. Sally told me. She said Martha is a wreck.

PETER: How far along is it?

CAROL: He's starting chemo.

PETER: That's a shame.

CAROL: I told her if there was anything we could do.

PETER: Good.

CAROL: *(Pause)* Finish your salad. You don't eat enough greens, Peter. *(Beat)* Oh, and you know who I heard is getting divorced?

PETER: Nothing but good news, tonight.

CAROL: Don't you want to know who?

PETER: Okay, who?

CAROL: Mike and Ann. You want to know why?

PETER: Why?

CAROL: Mike was having an affair...with a man.

PETER: I was always unsure about him.

CAROL: And guess what else? One of our friends is having a baby.

PETER: Good Lord.

CAROL: Lorraine.

PETER: She's gotta be fifty.

CAROL: Can you imagine? Makes our life seem uneventful.

PETER: Want a baby?

CAROL: No.

PETER: Cancer?

CAROL: Of course not. *(Beat)* Maybe an affair.

PETER: *(Sitting at the computer)* You get to have one I get to have one.

CAROL: Ha-ha. What are you doing?

PETER: I'm getting on the laptop to find some comparables.

CAROL: How are you going to do that?

PETER: Allegheny County Assessment Page, baby. Everything you wanted to know about all your neighbors, including what they paid in taxes. You know that big house on the corner, just sold last month? You know how much they paid for it? One dollar. With love and affection. I wish somebody would love me like that.

CAROL: I was planning to get on the laptop before Morgan got home.

PETER: Have you seen how much they've assessed us for? Our taxes could go up a hundred and fifty percent. You can say goodbye to your italian marble island if we don't win this appeal.

CAROL: All right all right, but then I'm getting on next.

PETER: (*Sitting down to the laptop*) Don't worry, your little chatterboxes will still be in their rooms by the time I'm done. Not that they ever leave.

CAROL: Just because you don't have any friends.

PETER: I have friends, just not imaginary ones.

CAROL: They're not imaginary, they just live in cyberspace. They're "cyber-friends."

PETER: I can't imagine what you talk about all night.

(PETER *turns on the computer,* CAROL *continues.*)

CAROL: Right now it's "American Politics."

PETER: (*Bursts out laughing*) That's the funniest thing I heard all week.

CAROL: Why? I have opinions.

PETER: Oh I know you do. Just not about politics.

CAROL: This one is a little boring. But we talk about other things too. Like our families, and everything. Just hurry up. (*She goes back to cleaning, sweeping around him.*) We must be old. Used to be if she was out of the house for more than an hour we'd be on the floor fighting to see who could get our pants off first, now we fight each other to sit in front of that computer.

PETER: You want to have sex first?

CAROL: That's all right. But I'll be too tired later.

PETER: Are you saying you want to have sex or you don't want to have sex?

CAROL: The mood is completely wrong now, just do what you have to do and I'll sign on after you.

PETER: Okay. *(Pause as he continues on computer.)*

CAROL: We can have sex in our great room after she goes to college.

PETER: I'm signing off.

CAROL: No, no, no, it's all right.

PETER: Tell me what you want, because if I'm supposed to guess I know I'm gonna get it wrong. Sex or no sex?

CAROL: I'm too tired already. Go ahead, do your computer. No sex.

PETER: Regularguy8762 is signing on...now.

CAROL: Then me. *(Pause. Then, she resumes cleaning/straightening.)* When I think about getting "old" I think about my Aunt Tessie. As long as I knew her she was old. Her hair was gray, the texture of steel wool, she was covered in wrinkles and bent over with an osteoporosis hump, which she tried to camouflage with festive designs.

PETER: *(Mostly focused on the computer)* Ew.

CAROL: The hump isn't what bothers me.

PETER: It bothers me.

CAROL: It's the clothes. How does that happen? One day you wake up and you're wearing polyester stretch pants and flowery blouses. I checked my closet this afternoon and you know what I found?

PETER: Aunt Tessie?

CAROL: Her wardrobe.

PETER: That's what this is about, there's a sale at Kaufmann's.

CAROL: One day your polyester wardrobe matches your hairstyle and your sensible shoes match the way you walk and your lavender perfume matches the way you think, then I'm an old lady and I can't remember how I got there and you're stuck with me. And yes there is a sale.

PETER: Knew it.

CAROL: But that isn't what this is about. This is the kind of things we talk about in my chatroom. This is my chatroom time now.

PETER: I'm looking forward to being an old man. I'll be retired. I'll sleep in. Read the entire newspaper in the bathroom. Spend the mornings playing golf and the afternoons online checking my stats.

CAROL: Sounds like a blast.

PETER: You grow old the way you want; I'll grow old the way I want.

CAROL: But it's boring, Peter. It's boring for me to watch you grow old like that.

PETER: Hey, no one's stopping you if you want to read the newspaper in the bathroom, now that we have two and a half bathrooms.

(Pause. PETER is focused on the screen. CAROL watches him a moment)

CAROL: Morgan is going to be leaving our house in the next twelve months for college. Doesn't that make you feel anything?

PETER: Poorer?

CAROL: Desperate. That's how it makes me feel.

PETER: That's crazy.

CAROL: Thank you.

PETER: You should be happy; you finally have your freedom back.

CAROL: To do what? Stare at the back of your head till one of us keels over.

PETER: To do what you want. Get a job. You like renovating kitchens, hire yourself out as a designer. Or take a page from your daughter's book and do something useful: volunteer. There's a lot you could do.

CAROL: No, no, no, that's not what I want. I don't want to work. I want—. I want—. I want to travel.

PETER: Okay. We'll go to Florida this winter.

CAROL: Oh God no. I'm talking about *traveling*. I'm talking about *adventure*. Like going on a Safari.

PETER: You're talking ten thousand dollars apiece.

CAROL: But it would be exciting.

PETER: Hey yeah we can go to Burundi, they almost had a coup the other day, and we missed it. Maybe we can go to Rwanda now that all those Hutus and Tutus are in jail.

CAROL: Forget Africa. How about Europe? I really want to go to Paris or Rome or Venice. Let's go to Paris before I'm an old lady in polyester and you're completely bald and all hope for romance between us is gone.

PETER: What do you mean, bald?

CAROL: You've got a bald spot, oh come on, you can't tell me you didn't know.

PETER: Where?

CAROL: Right there. (*Pokes his head*)

PETER: That's a part.

CAROL: At the back of your head?

PETER: You want me to get off the computer, just say so.

CAROL: I don't care if you're going bald, Peter. I care whether or not there's any passion left between us.

PETER: And we have to spend thousands of dollars in Europe to find that out? I thought when I got married it would be free.

CAROL: That's below the belt.

PETER: Like calling me bald?

CAROL: I'm getting ready for bed, tell me when you're off the computer. *(She exits.)*

PETER: *(Calling off to her)*

Sense of humor check.

(The light fades, PETER remains in front of computer)

(Light on PETER. The glow of the computer screen on his face)

PETER: When I dream, I'm being chased by a wild animal along dark twisted streets. It's breath stinks and just when I think I've lost it, I smell it, breathing down my neck again. I don't know what it is, a tiger, a dragon, something hideous and relentless like the IRS, but I can't bring myself to turn around and face what it is. Because I know I'm dreaming, I know that as long as I keep running, eventually, I am going to wake up, and then, I trip—

(Black out. Lights immediately up on:)

Scene Three

*(Night. CAROL alone at the computer. She has
signed on and starts typing. Lights up slowly on
TALL+DARK+HANDSOME at his computer. He is dressed
in black jeans and black tee shirt, barefoot, slightly non
descript. He is both sexy and strange in a boyish way but
morphs as the scene evolves into CAROL's idea of him)*

CAROL: Hi. Anybody there?

TALL+DARK+HANDSOME: TALL PLUS DARK PLUS
HANDSOME here. Missed you in the chat tonight,
COOLBREEZE. "Wink."

CAROL: Had a fight with the husband. L O L.

TALL+DARK+HANDSOME: Anything serious?

CAROL: No. Yes. The usual.

TALL+DARK+HANDSOME: Sorry.

CAROL: Don't be. "Smiley face."

TALL+DARK+HANDSOME: "Smiley face."

CAROL: What was the subject in the room tonight?

TALL+DARK+HANDSOME: "Are We the Police Men
of the World?" But nobody had anything to say.
Just the usual hugging and sending smiley faces.
I'm not against the smiley faces, but I like to move
beyond them. I need a new room. I miss the deep
conversations.

CAROL: I know what you mean. I'm thinking about
changing rooms too. Maybe something to do with
travel. Do you like to travel?

TALL+DARK+HANDSOME: It's my raison d'etre.

CAROL: *(To herself)* Is that a yes or a no? *(Types)* Ever
been to Africa?

TALL+DARK+HANDSOME: No, but I've been to South America hunting orchids for a wholesaler in SoHo.

CAROL: Really?

TALL+DARK+HANDSOME: I Love Orchids. Do you know an orchid has both male and female sex organs and is one of the few organisms that can fertilize itself.

CAROL: Didn't know that.

TALL+DARK+HANDSOME: Now you know. My apartment is full of orchids. Partly because you can't kill one, they are very hardy plants, they can grow anywhere, in anything, they need very little, I mean you have to want to kill this plant. L O L.

CAROL: L O L

TALL+DARK+HANDSOME: I also find them incredibly sexy. How about you?

CAROL: I think they're very beautiful.

TALL+DARK+HANDSOME: No, I meant you. Coolbreeze. That's a very sexy screen name.

CAROL: *(To herself)* Excuse me? *(Types)* And what about TALL+DARK+HANDSOME? Nothing left to the imagination there.

TALL+DARK+HANDSOME: Au contraire.

CAROL: *(To herself)* What is he, French?

(TALL+DARK+HANDSOME *leaves his space and enters hers at this point, although he is still in his cyber reality. Coming towards* CAROL)

TALL+DARK+HANDSOME: You don't know whether I'm telling the truth or not. All I give you is the opportunity to create an image, same as Coolbreeze which for me conjures up images of…key west…naked beaches…orchids in the amazon and you blowing in my ear.

CAROL: *(She gasps; then types.)* L O L. *(To herself)* Tall, dark, handsome and...french?

*(*TALL+DARK+HANDSOME *begins speaking in a French accent for the rest of this scene only.)*

TALL+DARK+HANDSOME: Is this the first time we've ever had a private chat?

CAROL: I think so...

TALL+DARK+HANDSOME: What should we do then?

CAROL: Aren't we...chatting?

TALL+DARK+HANDSOME: What if we did something more...?

CAROL: *(Pause)* Like...

TALL+DARK+HANDSOME: Like come closer...come on... *(He speaks what he is "typing".)* COOLBREEZE walks into a room softly lit with candles where TALL+DARK+HANDSOME has been waiting for her all night...

CAROL: *(To herself)* Oh.

TALL+DARK+HANDSOME: *(Beat)* Your turn.

(Lights quickly to black)

Scene Four

(Morning. MORGAN *enters and sees* CAROL *asleep in a chair pulled up to the kitchen table, the computer is still on.* MORGAN *begins banging around making coffee.* CAROL *wakes up, checks screen, starts to shut it off.)*

CAROL: There you are.

MORGAN: Don't shut down! I want to check my mail.

CAROL: I didn't hear you come in last night.

MORGAN: I didn't. You and Dad have a fight?

CAROL: What do you mean, you didn't?

MORGAN: It got late so I spent the night at Kristen's.

CAROL: You need to call when you do that.

MORGAN: I did call, the line was busy. One more reason to get another phone line.

CAROL: Forget it.

MORGAN: You guys not sleeping together anymore?

CAROL: Excuse me. I was waiting for you, for your information.

MORGAN: Okay. I'm sorry I didn't call. Excuse me.

(MORGAN *sits in front of the computer*)

CAROL: A better use of your time would be to start those essays for your college applications—

MORGAN: *(Signing onto the computer)* I know, I know, I am working on them, subconsciously, okay, every second that I breathe I am contemplating my "goals and dreams" for the future, *or* "where I see myself in five years" while I do other things more pressing at the moment.

CAROL: Like email.

MORGAN: Like changing the world, Mom.

CAROL: How was your meeting?

MORGAN: You don't care.

CAROL: I just asked you, didn't I?

MORGAN: You "care" in that you "care" about me, but as far as what the meeting was about, you don't care.

CAROL: It was something political, right?

MORGAN: That's right, Mom.

CAROL: Well in between your political activities you better get started on those applications, because applying early increases your chances of getting into the school you want.

MORGAN: Mom, did you sign that forward I sent you?

CAROL: What forward?

MORGAN: The forward calling for an end to the inhumane treatment of women in Afghanistan?

CAROL: No, I didn't sign it.

MORGAN: Did you send it back to me then?

CAROL: Oh, I don't know.

MORGAN: I don't have it in my mailbox.

CAROL: Then I guess I didn't.

MORGAN: Did you save it?

CAROL: I guess I deleted it.

MORGAN: What??

CAROL: Morgan, I don't have time for those endless emails you're always sending me.

MORGAN: And you claim to be interested in what I'm doing? I bet you didn't even read it.

CAROL: I read it.

MORGAN: And? *(Beat)* Are you not horrified by what's happening to those women? They can't go to school, they can't receive medical treatment, they can't feed their children, because they can't work or even beg in the streets. They are being systematically killed if they don't stay hidden in their houses. A woman driving down the street was pulled from her car and stoned to death by a group of men because her arm was showing.

CAROL: *(Overlapping)* I read it Morgan. What can I say, I feel sorry for those women.

MORGAN: It's not just about women. They blew up the Bamiyan Buddahs and you don't even care.

CAROL: I don't even know what they are.

MORGAN: They are just giant religious icons for an entire culture. Women and Art. That's what they hate. And that's just the beginning, they'll be after everybody sooner or later, while people like you sit and watch it on T V.

CAROL: When did this happen?

MORGAN: Months ago, Mom. They blew them up in March, which you would know if you ever read your mail. I sent you an email when it happened. You must have deleted that too.

CAROL: I don't see how signing an email is going to change anything.

MORGAN: No you wouldn't. You're a Wal-mart shopper.

CAROL: What is that supposed to mean?

MORGAN: It means you don't care about the truth behind things.

CAROL: I like shopping at Walmart. They have low prices. I don't care if they are politically inconvenient—

MORGAN: Try morally bankrupt—

CAROL: It's cheap that's why I shop there. And that's why everybody else does too.

MORGAN: What's cheap to you are these women's lives. You couldn't even lift a finger.

CAROL: I did lift a finger; I deleted it.

MORGAN: All the names on that petition are now lost, I specifically said to send it back to me if you weren't—

CAROL: Oh come on, everyone deletes those things.

MORGAN: I *don't*. My friends don't. The people I communicate with all over the world don't.

CAROL: Even if it got to someone who could do something about it, they would delete it because they don't care either.

MORGAN: They should.

CAROL: Of course they should, but they don't, that's reality.

MORGAN: And you know all about reality.

CAROL: What am I supposed to do, Morgan? Go to Afghanistan and personally wage war against all the stone-throwing icon destroying men? I have a life to live.

MORGAN: Yeah. Renovating your kitchen for the hundredth time.

CAROL: Have I redone this kitchen ninety-nine times?

(MORGAN *turns away from computer to face* CAROL.)

MORGAN: *(Calmly)* What is the purpose of a kitchen?

CAROL: The Purpose? To cook food.

MORGAN: But you never cook.

CAROL: I cooked last night.

MORGAN: Once in a hundred years.

CAROL: We are in the midst of renovations so I can cook *every night*, that's the point.

MORGAN: There is no point to your life, Mom: that's the point.

CAROL: *(Drinking her coffee, weary)* It's an ordinary life, Morgan.

MORGAN: There is a whole world of people out there, *(Gesturing toward computer)* that for them, the way we live is shameful.

CAROL: Because I want an updated kitchen?

MORGAN: The way we *waste*. The way we *consume*. *Shopping* for cheap crap at Walmart, while "little brown people" die working in factories for pennies so we can re-do a perfectly good kitchen that we don't even use because—

CAROL: *(Overlapping)* I need more cabinet space!

MORGAN: But it never satisfies, Mom, that's why you have to keep doing it. The only thing that satisfies is helping other people, but you have no idea about that because your life is so small.

CAROL: Excuse me. I help people. I help you. I help your father and your grandparents and I help the neighbors, sometimes.

MORGAN: That's good, but our responsibilities don't end there.

CAROL: My job is not to right every wrong in the world.

MORGAN: Then what is your job?

(Pause)

CAROL: *(Stumped)* I quit my job seventeen years ago so I could take care of my family, and make us all happy.

MORGAN: Happiness is your job?

CAROL: Yes, why not?

MORGAN: That is the most selfish thing I've heard in my life. It's time for a new job, Mom.

CAROL: Why? That's what you're doing. All your politics, you do for yourself.

MORGAN: Excuse me, I have to take a shower, then I'm going back to Kristen's where we will be writing letters to save a woman's life, while you pick out little knobs for your cabinets.

((MORGAN collides with PETER as he enters, dressed for work, a laptop over his shoulder MORGAN exits.)

PETER: Having a heart to heart?

CAROL: Just doing my job: making everybody happy. We're not political people. How did we make her?

PETER: Speak for yourself. I like to keep informed on the issues... Is there coffee made?

CAROL: Morgan made it.

PETER: I'll stop at Starbucks on the way to work.

(Pause. Their spat last night in the air between them.)

PETER: I'm gonna be late tonight. Working on the appeal at the office. Then I'm getting my hair cut. Don't bother making dinner for me. I'll grab something out.

CAROL: Fine.

PETER: Don't be mad all day.

CAROL: I'm not mad. You're the one's mad.

PETER: I could see that you were intent on having an argument and I chose to stay out of your way.

CAROL: That's very patronizing.

PETER: No, it's actually very loving. And mature. You should try it. *(Kisses her on the head)* Have a good day. And don't fight with Morgan.

CAROL: She fights with me.

PETER: If I get a chance I'll call a financial planner today. Maybe once we get her first year of college behind us, we could go some place. How's that?

CAROL: What do I do in the meantime?

PETER: Put the dishes back in the cabinets? Go shopping? Or...take a day off? *(As he exits)* I'm taking the Lexus. The Explorer needs gas. If you go shopping put it on the credit card...

CAROL: *(To him, gone)* Love you too. *(She sits for a moment, then turns on computer.)*

(Fade out)

Scene Five

(Sound of running water. MORGAN *appears in a bathrobe holding a towel. She is about to take a shower. [Note: we might see her behind a scrim with voiceover or just spotlight. Keep it simple])*

MORGAN: I have a recurring dream inspired by this insane fairytale my mother read to me one night when I was seven. I'm in a shoe store and this witch of a woman is trying to convince me to buy these red shoes, like Dorothy's from *The Wizard of Oz.* There is no excuse for these shoes. They're not punky or retro or anything, they are just evil. But the witch won't get off my back, so I try them on against my better judgement. Now I can't get them off, and go dancing out of the store and down the street till I get downtown to the Point, where the three rivers meet; where the big fountain is. The shoes are biting into my feet and they're bleeding, and I'm leaving little bloody footprints all around the fountain till the shoes decide to take me straight into the water which at this point is a poisonous confluence of slime. And as I go deeper and deeper, I am slowly dissolving as I merge with the rivers and the slime and then I wake up.

(Sound of water stops.)

MORGAN: *(Screaming)* AHHH! MOM WHAT HAPPENED TO ALL THE HOT WATER???

(Lights out, up immediately on next scene)

Scene Six

(Later than night: CAROL *alone at the computer/*
TALL+DARK+HANDSOME *is at his computer. He has lost*
the French accent, but he is evolving more into CAROL'*s*
idealized version of TALL+DARK+HANDSOME.*)*

CAROL: And then the hot water heater broke only the
plumber knows why. The basement flooded while
my daughter, who was taking a shower, is screaming.
The workmen are pounding on the door, so I run
upstairs from the basement to let them in when some
pipe under the sink bursts. By now the dishwasher is
overflowing, and the cat is crying. When I look down,
Snowball is projectile vomiting across the kitchen
floor, so now I've got to take the animal to the vet
and all I want to do is get in the car and drive off the
Birmingham Bridge—

TALL+DARK+HANDSOME: Sounds like a bad day.

CAROL: Am I complaining?

TALL+DARK+HANDSOME: *(Says)* Yes. *(Types)* Not at all.

CAROL: I feel like I'm becoming invisible. I look in the
mirror and I don't see a forty—delete—a woman in
her late—delete—thirties, I see a young girl caught
in a train wreck. Not that I look like a train wreck,
L O L, I think I've kept my figure, I do my step aerobics
every single damn day, it's just that I don't know how
I got from there to here, deep down I still feel like I'm
seventeen. And I never imagined then that this is what
my life would be like now.

TALL+DARK+HANDSOME: Did you ever want to get out
of it?

CAROL: Out of what?

TALL+DARK+HANDSOME: Your domestic constraints.

CAROL: No, of course not. I hope I didn't give you the wrong idea. Just because we, "talked" the other night, it doesn't mean I want to leave my husband. L O L.

TALL+DARK+HANDSOME: I'm not judging you.

CAROL: I love my family.

TALL+DARK+HANDSOME: Hmm-hmm.

CAROL: I've always put them first. I've sacrificed everything for our home, my husband, our child. I never wanted anything else.

TALL+DARK+HANDSOME: What about your husband?

CAROL: What about him?

TALL+DARK+HANDSOME: Still in love with him?

CAROL: I love him.

TALL+DARK+HANDSOME: That's not what I asked.

CAROL: I know what you asked and that's a stupid question. Peter is like an arm or a leg I couldn't live without him.

TALL+DARK+HANDSOME: You can live without an arm or a leg.

CAROL: He's like my heart beating in my chest.

TALL+DARK+HANDSOME: Yes yes I know but does he satisfy you? *(Brief pause)* Sex-u-al-ly.

CAROL: Not lately.

TALL+DARK+HANDSOME: What do you dream about?

CAROL: I haven't had a dream I remember since I was seventeen.

(Pause)

TALL+DARK+HANDSOME: What do you miss the most about being seventeen?

CAROL: Omigod.

TALL+DARK+HANDSOME: Be specific.

CAROL: It's a feeling. A restless feeling, like excitement, or fear, but good fear. Like I'm on the verge of something incredible but unknown; like on the first day of spring when you can't feel the weather on your skin because it's just perfect, and there's a clear blue sky, and then out of nowhere comes a cool breeze that I can feel—. Listen to me, I'm a poet.

TALL+DARK+HANDSOME: Don't stop.

CAROL: I can feel it with my whole body.

TALL+DARK+HANDSOME: Give it a name.

CAROL: Possibility.

TALL+DARK+HANDSOME: *(To himself)* No more talking. *(To her)* Remember the other night? Let's do that again only this time when I describe how I'm going to touch you, you're going to feel me touch you.

CAROL: How?

TALL+DARK+HANDSOME: By touching yourself when I do.

CAROL: What?

TALL+DARK+HANDSOME: I'm gonna satisfy you like old what's his name never could.

(Lights dim as CAROL *begins having internet sex with* TALL+DARK+HANDSOME. *We see it from the point of view of her imagination. They leave their computers to meet in a cyber reality of their minds.)*

(While this is going on, PETER *is on his computer at the office, talking online to a sympathetic ear, and* MORGAN *appears online, instant messaging.)*

(All this is happening at once. As each one types/talks/sends their messages, they alternate with each other, appearing in spots or some other lighting convention to separate/highlight

them in their particular cyber/spaces. CAROL *and* TED *should be physically touching each other as they make "wild love")*

PETER: So much un-full-fill-ment. So much I was supposed to do by now. How did my life become so mediocre?

MORGAN: I'm seventeen, and I'm supposed to make decisions that are going to affect the rest of my life. How can I know now what I'll want later?

*(*CAROL *begins to quietly vocalize.)*

PETER: No, no, I'm not unhappy.

MORGAN: When I pretend to want what everybody else wants, I feel like a stereotype of myself.

PETER: Although my wife is.

*(*CAROL *gets louder.)*

MORGAN: The sportsjock boyfriend ivy league school big wedding house in the burbs two point five kids and a minivan.

PETER: Unhappy. *Unhappy.*

CAROL: *(As their passion intensifies)*

Omigod. Keep typing, keep typing.

MORGAN: I'm sorry. I want a real life not a commercial for that life. And I want to be *awake* for it.

PETER: I look at her and think; I've given you everything you wanted, why are you reneging on our contract.

MORGAN: I look around me and everybody is sleepwalking through their lives. Their eyes are open, they're going to work, driving cars, shopping, renovating kitchens, but nothing seems to penetrate. I'm beginning to realize that most people are just not aware of what's going on in the real world.

PETER: The contract that said, if I did my part and you did yours, by now we should be living happily ever after.

(CAROL *is beginning to climax.*)

MORGAN: If they want something it's at Walmart, if they feel something, it's a Walmart emotion, if they have a political opinion, if they didn't buy it on sale at Walmart, they saw it sandwiched between commercials on C N N. I mean get real—

PETER: I mean, here I am talking to you, a complete stranger, about the intimate workings of my marriage, when I should be confronting her. Or talking. I'm not accusing her of anything. I don't think. But something is going on, or is about to, I can feel it.

(CAROL *climaxes through* MORGAN's *next speech.*)

MORGAN: I feel like running through the streets shouting at everyone: *wake up the sky is falling take cover do something!*

(*Pause, they are all four quiet, then:*)

PETER: Maybe everyone feels like this in their late forties?

MORGAN: But no one would hear me because they prefer to live in denial.

(CAROL *kisses* TALL+DARK+HANDSOME's *head.*)

PETER: You don't? Did all your dreams come true?

MORGAN: Or maybe it's because they're all *deaf!*

PETER: Are you married?

MORGAN: *Stone.*

PETER: Whining?

MORGAN: *Deaf.*

PETER: Because I've got a problem, that makes me a whiner? Hey I am still the dutiful husband, who goes to work, makes the money, pays the bills, diversifies his portfolio, elects politicians who promise to lower his taxes but who instead over-inflates the value of his house, thereby raising his property taxes in a plan called *how to eradicate the Pittsburgh taxbase.*

MORGAN: I want to figure out how to live my own life—

PETER: How do they sleep at night?

MORGAN: And be AWARE that I'm living it, at the same time.

(TALL kisses CAROL goodbye, he disappears, back to his own computer.)

PETER: But I'm going to fight it.

MORGAN: Is that so much to ask?

PETER: If that makes me a whiner, so be it.

(Pause)

CAROL: *(Typing)* When can I—can we—do that again?

(Lights shift)

Scene Seven

(August 2001. Rain. CAROL is concentrating on the computer screen. A large orchid sits nearby. A huge clap of thunder. MORGAN is peering over CAROL's shoulder.)

CAROL: Do you need something?

MORGAN: Daddy's calling you. Can't you hear him?

(PETER dashes into the kitchen grabbing pots and pans.)

PETER: GET A PAN, A BUCKET ANYTHING, THE DAMN ROOF IS COLLAPSING.

CAROL: What's the matter? What's wrong with the roof?

MORGAN: The roof is leaking.

PETER: IT'S NOT A ROOF IT'S A SIEVE. The water is pouring in; it's flooding the bedroom.

CAROL: What do you want me to do about it?

PETER: Maybe get off the damn computer and help me?

CAROL: Oh, all right. Let me just finish what I'm doing and I'll get off, okay?

PETER: I've got to leave in fifteen minutes, if you miss your slot they reschedule you, I won't get to make my appeal til after September. Morgan, don't we have one of those cameras, what the hell are they called, they develop right away.

MORGAN: I don't know.

PETER: *(Running back upstairs)* This sucks, but I can use it! I'VE JUST GOT TO DOCUMENT IT!

CAROL: Why is everything a crisis in this house? What are you staring at?

MORGAN: Aren't you going to help him?

CAROL: In a minute. Can't I have two minutes to myself in this house?

MORGAN: Actually you've been on there for an hour.

CAROL: You haven't been up an hour, how do you know?

MORGAN: Mom, don't confuse reality with the internet.

CAROL: What are you talking about?

MORGAN: I know how tempting it is, because I been there done that already.

CAROL: Been there done what?

MORGAN: Confused reality with the Land of Oz. It happens to everybody when they first get online.

CAROL: I don't know what you're talking about.

MORGAN: You're going along lahdeedah in your normal Kansean existence when out of nowhere this technology descends on you like a tornado. You get swept up in it and it takes you where *it* wants to. Then before you know it, you find yourself in a strange place called a *chatroom* with all these wild characters and you keep getting drawn further in by the promise of what's down that yellow brick road. You're thinking this is great, I get to wear the magic ruby slippers and chat with all these cool people and you start to think, hey, this is where I can make all my dreams come true.

PETER: *(Off)* SHIT! SHIT! CAROL CAN YOU COME HELP ME PLEASE?

(MORGAN watches as CAROL ignores PETER.)

PETER: *(To himself)* WHY WON'T ANYONE HELP ME?

MORGAN: What are you doing?

CAROL: I'm checking fares, do you mind?

MORGAN: Going somewhere?

CAROL: I'm window shopping. In case, God forbid, I should ever actually go somewhere. *(Beat)* Research, okay?

MORGAN: It's worse than I thought. Face it Mom, you're addicted.

CAROL: I am not.

MORGAN: I don't blame you. Given the choice between Oz and Kansas who wouldn't take Oz. Oz is a colorful place inhabited by happy mindless munchkins where everybody sings and dances. There's a funny well meaning scarecrow, a harmless cowardly lion and a

weepy tin man. Kansas is gray, boring, predictable,
and the roof leaks.

(Thunder rain and PETER *screaming)*

PETER: *(Off)* CAROL WHERE ARE ALL THE TOWELS?

CAROL: TAKE THE DIRTY ONES FROM THE
HAMPER IN THE BATHROOM.

MORGAN: But there's also flying monkeys and violent
trees and a wicked witch who would kill you as soon
as look at you so you have to stay awake when you're
crossing that field of poppies because not everything is
what it seems.

CAROL: *(Thrusts an armload of kitchen tea towels at*
MORGAN*)* Here bring these towels up to your father.

MORGAN: *(Immediately putting down the towels)* For
one thing there's a nerdy guy behind the curtain, he's
a geek, more than a little strange, and he's working
his smoke and mirrors hoping you stay focused on
the image he's projecting on the screen because he
has absolutely no power. It's your willingness to be
deceived by him that makes him powerful.

CAROL: I have absolutely no idea what you are
rambling on about.

MORGAN: Look behind the curtain. That's all I'm
saying. *(She sits in front of the computer.)*

CAROL: Work on your essay before you do anything
else. And what about your S A Ts, hmm? What did I
get that tutor for if you're never going to study for it?
Morgan, it's August 10th. School starts in three weeks,
you better get your act together, miss.

MORGAN: See, Mom, you've got to learn how to use the
internet, not be used by it.

CAROL: Oh really.

MORGAN: It's a tool, to help you connect, communicate, find out information, but it shouldn't be an end in itself.

CAROL: *(Calling upstairs)* PETER DO YOU STILL NEED THESE TOWELS??

MORGAN: There are certain rules: number one: never give anyone your real name. Never tell anyone where you live and never give out your phone number.

CAROL: I think I'm the mother.

MORGAN: And don't forget your wedding vows.

CAROL: All right Morgan, enough. What are you getting at?

MORGAN: Tall plus Dark plus Handsome doesn't always add up to what's behind the curtain.

CAROL: *(Pause)* Have you been reading my email?

MORGAN: Hard not to. You left it on the screen for the world to see. Explained a lot.

CAROL: That was—that was a book. A book I'm writing.

MORGAN: Trashy romance novel.

CAROL: Does everyone have to be Herman Melville?

MORGAN: Has Dad read it?

PETER: *(Entering soaking wet)* Read what?

CAROL: Peter. Here are the towels.

MORGAN: Mom's writing a book. She's a novelist now.

PETER: I don't like to get between Mom and her creativity. Right now I've got to build an Ark.

CAROL: Is everything wet up there?

PETER: Let me put it this way. We should sleep in the backyard tonight. The grass will be dryer.

CAROL: You want me to bring up these towels?

PETER: Can you hurry up there, Princess? Your old man's got to get on line to find blueprints for an Ark.

MORGAN: I just got on.

PETER: Forget it. I don't have time anyway. I've got to be downtown in ten minutes. They'll have to lower that assessment now since we don't have a roof. *(He grabs a stack of papers near computer)*

CAROL: Don't you want some dry clothes?

PETER: No, they'll want evidence.

MORGAN: Maybe you should kiss your wife goodbye.

CAROL: Should I mop up up there?

PETER: Just line the animals up two by two; I'll take care of it when I get home.

CAROL: That joke is old already Peter.

PETER: *(Turning on her)* Do whatever you want. I was calling you and calling you and you couldn't get up off your ass to help me, now everything is soaked, the rug is squelching and I am late for my appeal. But now I have a real case. Ironic, isn't it?

(PETER exits. Silence between the two women)

MORGAN: *(She turns back to the computer.)* Oh my God. Did you know we bombed "air defense targets" in Southern Iraq today. See these are the kinds of things you don't notice when you're hanging out in Oz.

CAROL: You've got enough to do worrying about yourself, like what school is going to accept you if you can't even get the applications filled out. Why would they want someone who takes an entire summer to write a two hundred word essay, if the slightest little thing you see on the computer is going to distract you from what's important? Like getting a high score on the SATS so you can get into a decent school?? So just, worry about yourself.

MORGAN: What if I don't want the ordinary nine-to-five-life-in-the- suburbs-get-a-job-working-for-an-existence you're offering me? What if I want to discover what my dreams are, instead of writing them out in two hundred words or less? What if I want more out of life than what you settled for?

CAROL: You are seventeen years old, you have no idea what you want out of life.

MORGAN: You're exactly right. Which is why I am not going to college.

CAROL: Oh you're going. You don't have a choice about that.

MORGAN: I've already made my decision, Mom. It's all over but the screaming.

CAROL: I invested a lot in you. Between after school art and music classes and dance on Saturdays and math tutoring and chess club and soccer every damn weekend—don't roll your eyes at me—and summer science camps and private school and college preparation counseling. I didn't pour all that time and money into you so you could end up being a Stay At Home Mom.

MORGAN: I said I didn't want to go to college, not that I was planning to throw my life away.

CAROL: *(That hurt)* I just want you to be happy, that's all.

MORGAN: Happiness, happiness, I'm sick of all this talk of happiness. What the hell is happiness? I don't believe in happiness, Mom.

CAROL: Is that how your generation feels, well that's depressing.

MORGAN: No, happiness is depressing. I want something more.

CAROL: What more is there?

MORGAN: I want to be useful.

CAROL: Then be a social worker. But go to college first.

MORGAN: I want to live a moral life.

CAROL: Then be a nun.

MORGAN: I want to live an authentic life, a truthful life, and not a lie.

CAROL: *(Shouting)* THEN DO IT!

MORGAN: *(Shouting back)* OKAY I WILL!

CAROL: BUT YOU'LL GO TO COLLEGE FIRST because if I have to I will write that damn essay for you.

MORGAN: Of course you will, like you always do. Tell me what my dreams are.

CAROL: Because you wait and wait and wait until the last minute because you know in the end I'll do it.

MORGAN: You can't live my life for me anymore, Mom. You gotta stop sometime!

CAROL: I'm not trying to live your life for you; I'm trying to teach you responsibility.

MORGAN: Everything you do is vicarious. You live through me or Dad, or on the computer pretending you're Dorothy. I don't think you're in the position to teach me anything about real life or responsibility. What about your responsibility to the planet? To humanity? Or how about to your own soul?

CAROL: Every generation thinks it's going to change the world, you are not the first, but you'll grow up and you'll see it can't be done.

(CAROL grabs MORGAN's arm, as she turns away.)

The only thing you can do is take care of yourself, and that's what I'm trying to help you do. Go to college, get an education, get a job. Then you can do what you want—

(MORGAN *pulls away,* CAROL *pursues.*)

CAROL: But I can see already what's going to happen to you. Cause you won't think any more than I did. You'll meet some guy, fall in love and get married. And then everything you want now will go out the window. Because you'll have kids and you won't have time for any of this nonsense anymore. (*She stands face to face* MORGAN.) Because you'll be just like me, Morgan, living day to day: going shopping, cooking meals, yes, cleaning the house, doing the laundry, taking the cat to the vet, taking care of everyone else, and there won't be time for any other nonsense, like worrying about who we're bombing. Because we are always bombing someone! And what you have to do today nibbles and nibbles and nibbles away until there's nothing left. (*It comes pouring out now.*) Your concept of the planet will shrink to the size of your kitchen island and humanity will be the people sitting around it who have hooked up their vacuum cleaners to your jugular and have sucked, sucked, sucked everything out until your soul has become as a dry as a desert.

(CAROL *bursts into tears.*)

MORGAN: That's scary, Mom.

CAROL: So don't talk to me about my soul.

MORGAN: I'm sorry I brought it up.

(MORGAN *exits.* CAROL *stops crying. SHE gets up wipes her eyes, blows her nose and sits down in front of the computer, signs on.*)

Scene Eight

(CAROL *is online with* TALL+DARK+HANDSOME)

CAROL: Hi. My name is Carol and I live in Pittsburgh.

TALL+DARK+HANDSOME: Hey Pittsburgh.

CAROL: "Hell with the lid off" is what they used to call it. *(Pause)* That's where I live. *(Pause)* Where do you live?

(Pause)

TALL+DARK+HANDSOME: The Emerald City.

CAROL: Haha. Really.

TALL+DARK+HANDSOME: Really. Otherwise known as New York New York.

CAROL: You're not French.

TALL+DARK+HANDSOME: Only in bed.

CAROL: Good. I could drive there. Meet you.

TALL+DARK+HANDSOME: Okay.

CAROL: Okay?

TALL+DARK+HANDSOME: Sure, why not. You like Thai?

CAROL: Sure why not?

TALL+DARK+HANDSOME:I'll take you to my favorite Thai place on Second Avenue.

CAROL: Yes!

TALL+DARK+HANDSOME: Jump into that minivansuvwhatever all terrain soccer mom vehicle you drive in hell and come to the lower east side. I'll take you out for some fabulous Thai.

CAROL: Yes! Yes!

TALL+DARK+HANDSOME: Of course we take a chance don't we?

CAROL: I don't understand.

TALL+DARK+HANDSOME:I don't want to rock your world.

CAROL: Rock it, rock it.

TALL+DARK+HANDSOME: What if you're three hundred pounds?

CAROL: I'm not. Are you?

TALL+DARK+HANDSOME: We risk losing everything we have.

CAROL: What do we have?

TALL+DARK+HANDSOME: Our fantasy.

CAROL: But what if we can make our fantasy real?

TALL+DARK+HANDSOME: It's real enough. Isn't that what makes it so great?

(TALL+DARK+HANDSOME *steps out of his world and into hers, behind her chair*)

TALL+DARK+HANDSOME:It's like a dream we never have to wake up from, there's no hesitation, no awkwardness in front of each other, we see straight into each other's minds. And in our minds there are no boundaries, no limits. When I touch you, I touch you exactly the way you want to be touched.

CAROL: I know.

TALL+DARK+HANDSOME: *(Taking her hands)* Our two dreams can be separate and yet together. No consequences.

CAROL: I know.

TALL+DARK+HANDSOME: *(He runs her hands down her body)* I just don't want to lose a good thing.

CAROL: Neither do I, but I want, I need an experience right now. The real thing.

TALL+DARK+HANDSOME: Okay. Come then. We'll go out and have some fabulous Thai food, with a Pinot Grigio, I think, nothing too heavy, then we'll go back to my place, with dusk falling through the skylight over the bed. At first we'll be unsure, embarrassed even, masked to each other for so long, hiding behind words, now about to expose ourselves in the flesh, you'll be trembling with anticipation and excitement and I will strip you naked, ready to explore you like an undiscovered continent.

CAROL: How's next week?

TALL+DARK+HANDSOME: I'm going to the beach for two weeks.

CAROL: I was hoping to come before September. My kid's got school and I need to—delete. How's Labor Day?

TALL+DARK+HANDSOME: I'm free the day after.

CAROL: I'll be there.

TALL+DARK+HANDSOME: September 4th, 2001. I'm writing it down. Now give me a little sugar to snack on till then.

(CAROL *starts typing when* PETER *walks in. He is still damp, carrying a folder stuffed with papers every which way.*)

(CAROL *gives him her attention, but she doesn't fully disengage from* TALL+DARK+HANDSOME *who is still hanging on the back of her chair molesting her from behind throughout this scene.*)

PETER: They think I'm a nutcase.

CAROL: Did you get the assessment lowered?

PETER: They don't tell you while your standing there. They listen, they ask stupid questions, they write down the incriminating things you say and then they argue with you, try to belittle you, make you realize you have no power.

CAROL: Did you tell them we don't have three bathrooms?

PETER: Yes I did but he argued with me. I said we have a plain old dinky bathroom on the second floor, and a tiny room on the first floor, not even a powder room, a pantry, not even a broom closet. And then he asks me about the one in the basement. A stinky little hole in the ground nobody actually uses. "It's called a Pittsburgh Toilet," I say, and he says, "I know, you live in Pittsburgh, that's why I know you have one." So I tell him "Okay, in "theory" I have three bathrooms" and he writes something down on his little pad. "Can we continue" he says, and I say "Yes, please, let's talk about the grade you gave my house. An A-." "How can you give a house an A-," I demand, "that has a roof like that." And he says, "I actually never saw your house." And I was like, "Why am I talking to you if you're not the assessor who saw it?" Then he tells me this long drawn out story about his brother in law who was out of work, and he filled in for him a couple of times when he had to go to a closing or something. And I have to "understand family" or maybe he said "the economy" and I was like, "Look, can I talk to you mano to mano?" I say, "We actually have a lot in common. You over assessed my house, and I over assessed my marriage.

CAROL: What are you talking about?

PETER: I say, "Of course a realtor stands to gain by inflating the market value of homes in his selling area, just as a husband stands to gain a good night's sleep by assuming he is happy in his domestic area," so we were on the same page finally. Although he was getting a little defensive, like you are, so I said, "Hey,

I am not accusing you of anything *intentional*, only that you can see how you might tip things a teensey weensey bit in your favor, maybe subconsciously, without realizing what you were doing."

CAROL: What does this have to do with me, Peter?

PETER: Not "me", Carol, "us", Carol. The metaphor is the marriage. So, I got his attention now and I continue.

(PETER *has* CAROL's *attention now too*)

PETER: "Faced with the results, you can see where you made a mistake, and once you see this plain as day, you can make adjustments for reality. You can lower my property taxes and I can fix my roof. Do you get the metaphor, now, Carol?

CAROL: I think you're mixing your metaphors, now, Peter.

PETER: The purpose of a marriage, besides working out some heavy duty karma, is to shelter and protect each other from what's outside. In other words it's supposed to be a good thing. Then he said to me, "Why don't you talk to your wife?" So I'm talking to you, Carol. *(Beat)* Is there somebody else?

CAROL: (TALL+DARK+HANDSOME *still behind her)* No.

(Pause)

PETER: What can I do to make you happy? Under a thousand dollars.

CAROL: I want to visit my parents in Florida, Labor Day weekend.

PETER: Done.

(The lights shift as all three access each other)

Scene Nine

(September 1, 2001. CAROL is re-packing a too full suitcase on the floor. A Kaufman's shopping bag lies next to it. MORGAN is holding the orchid.)

CAROL: Can you put that back in the bag, please?

MORGAN: If you're going to Florida to visit Grandma why can't I come?

CAROL: Because you have school starting on Tuesday and I won't be back by then.

MORGAN: But that's why I need you. School is starting. You've never not been here for the first day of school.

CAROL: You're a senior in high school. Need me to pack your lunch?

MORGAN: When are you coming back?

CAROL: A few days. When was the last time I went anywhere?

MORGAN: Never.

CAROL: Exactly.

MORGAN: If you're looking for room in that suitcase you can get rid of those red come fuck me shoes.

CAROL: Excuse me.

MORGAN: I'm sorry. *(She holds up the shoes with the tips of her fingers)* These shoes are hideous. I don't see why you're bringing them instead of your birkenstocks. That's what you normally wear at Grandma's.

CAROL: *(Repacking shoes)* I might take her out to a restaurant.

MORGAN: Are you going because of me?

CAROL: Why would this have anything to do with you?

MORGAN: Because we're always fighting and I "make your life a living hell." I'm quoting you.

CAROL: No, Morgan this has to do with me. For once.

MORGAN: Is this something to do with menopause?

CAROL: No.

MORGAN: Are you leaving Daddy?

CAROL: No.

MORGAN: It's that weird guy on the internet, isn't?

CAROL: Morgan, what I need right now is a little space.

(Pause)

MORGAN: Why are you bringing Grandma an orchid?

CAROL: She likes orchids.

MORGAN: They don't have orchids in Florida?

(Pause)

CAROL: Okay. I'm driving to New York City, to see the man I met on the internet. He's a friend, we're going to meet in person, since we've developed—a friendship— and we're gonna—do lunch.

MORGAN: Does Daddy know?

CAROL: No. Satisfied?

MORGAN: What if he's a whacko?

CAROL: He's not.

MORGAN: How do you know?

CAROL: I know.

MORGAN: But why do you have to meet him, you're a married woman.

CAROL: I'm not going to do anything *wrong* but obviously Daddy is not going to understand if I told him the truth.

MORGAN: *(Starting to cry)* But what if something happens to you! I'll feel guilty!

CAROL: *(Taking the orchid from* MORGAN *and re-packing it carefully in the shopping bag)*

Nothing is going to happen. That's the point, honey. Nothing ever happens to me. Okay, maybe this is bad what I'm doing, but I can't explain it to you because I can't fully explain it to myself. I've never been a role model for you, right? You're not going to throw your life away and be a Stay At Home Mom.

MORGAN: Mom, I didn't mean that.

CAROL: *(A blossom from the orchid comes off in her hand)* Oh, look the petals are falling off now! *(Tries to press it back on, throws it in bag with rest of plant)* Shit.

MORGAN: Why are you bringing this man an orchid?

*(*CAROL *gets her purse, finds her keys.)*

CAROL: You have your whole life ahead of you. I'm going away for just three days.

MORGAN: *(Pulling out a crumpled piece of paper)*

I wrote my essay, for my college applications, it's called "My Hopes and Dreams," want to hear it?

CAROL: Email it to me. *(Swinging her bag over her shoulder, suitcase in one hand, shopping bag in the another)* I'll read it when I get home.

*(*CAROL *exits. Fade to black)*

END OF ACT ONE

(Intermission if desired would be here)

ACT TWO

Scene Ten

(Pittsburgh. MORGAN *alone in the "great room", sitting at the center island in front of a laptop, typing)*

MORGAN: My mother has run away from home. She said she'd be gone three days; it's been a week. My father is in deep denial. But as weird as that is, I totally realize it's their drama. I've got my own. I wrote this boring little essay for my college applications, which I told my mother no one was ever going to read, but that she kept nagging at me to do. So I put down all of my hopes and dreams for the future, you know: I want world peace, equality for women, political freedom for all. *Words.* Nobody pays attention to words. If nobody reads them, they have absolutely *no effect.* So from now on I am going for *action.* I am going to *do. Something.* I'm not sure what yet. But it will be something BIG. I found a great website: *"Your bliss and how to follow it"* designed to help you discover your destiny. Okay, so I found out I don't belong in Pittsburgh. I'm more suited to the Pacific Northwest. Like Seattle or Tibet. I took the survey and it said I should be an environmental terrorist or a Buddhist nun. Either you are on your path to your bliss or you are totally *not.* It's a question of when I want to get on the path. I could finish senior year, or I can leave tomorrow. One thing I know is I'm not gonna be like my mother and wait forty years before I follow my heart's desire.

(MORGAN *grabs her backpack and exits*)
(*Lights quickly fade.*)

Scene Eleven

(*New York, New York. September 9, 2001. The "great room" has transformed into a funky downtown restaurant, very white, very spare, very cool.* CAROL *is sitting on a high stool at an impossibly tiny table. She is wearing the red shoes. The orchid is sticking out of the shopping bag, under her chair*)

(TED, *A K A* TALL+DARK+HANDSOME, *sits across from her, pouring more wine into her glass.*)

(CAROL *is laughing to cover embarrassment, or drunkenness*).

TED: You're blushing.

CAROL: Flushing. It's the wine. I'm not used to drinking this much with dinner—Ted. (*She bursts out laughing.*)

TED: What?

CAROL: I can't get used to calling you "Ted." I want to call you Tall plus Dark plus Handsome, or just "Tall."

TED: But I'm not "tall." (*If actor is tall, change to "I'm tall."*)

CAROL: Or Dark. (*If actor is dark, change to "and [or but] your dark." Laughing again*) For a brief period I thought you were tall, dark and french!

TED: What about Handsome? I'm fishing for a compliment here.

CAROL: (*Singsong*) Oh come on, you know you're not hard on the eyes.

TED: I'm still gonna call you Cool. It suits you.

CAROL: I don't mind.

TED: There's something honest about you, like the windows are open and a spring breeze is blowing in the curtains.

CAROL: Oh...you.

TED: No I mean it, you're a real person, you say what you mean, and you mean what you say.

CAROL: Not really. Hahaha. I mean not all the time. Who does that all the time?

TED: You said you were coming and here you are. In the flesh. Coolbreeze sitting next to Tall plus Dark plus Handsome.

CAROL: I almost changed my mind. It took me a week to get up the nerve to call you. I'd walk down your block, and then every time I passed your door, I'd just keep going.

TED: What do you mean keep going? Where'd you go?

CAROL: Everywhere! That Greyline is so convenient. One day I went downtown, ate in Chinatown and took the ferry to the statue of liberty, the next day I went to the top of the empire state building, rode all over midtown. I went to central park, up and down fifth avenue, finally I went and saw a show, something I never do, and it was surprisingly enjoyable, you know those Irish dancers, river something,

TED: Dance.

CAROL: Right. How fast they move their feet. Just amazing. Really.

TED: Did you go to the top of the Trade Center?

CAROL: I did not do that. The day I planned to do that, I decided life is too short, I'm just going to do it.

TED: If you want, I'll take you up there.

CAROL: Break every rule I ever followed my entire life, get off the bus and ring your bell.

TED: Well I'm impressed. *(Pause)* More wine?

CAROL: I think I've had enough.

TED: *(Pouring)* You're not driving that Tank back to Pittsburgh tonight.

CAROL: *(Drinking, laughing)* It's not a tank. It's a Ford Explorer.

TED: I'm proud to say I have never owned a car.

CAROL: Do you have a girlfriend?

TED: Nothing serious…at the moment.

CAROL: Ever been serious?

TED: I've been married. Does that count? When I was young.

CAROL: "When" you were young?

TED: Hey don't let this baby face fool ya. I was eighteen when I got married.

CAROL: That is young.

TED: She was a lot older than I was. Don't get me wrong, I love older women. But looking back I can't imagine what she saw in me.

CAROL: I can imagine.

TED: I was eighteen, she was thirty. What do you talk to an eighteen year old about when you're thirty?

CAROL: Sometimes what you talk about doesn't matter.

TED: Good talk can be just as erotic as good sex. We oughta know.

CAROL: Desire can be very…unpredictable.

(PETER enters as the owner, CAROL stares a moment at the resemblance, then avoids his eyes, let's TED do the talking.)

PETER/OWNER: Everything all right?

CAROL: Uh yeah.

TED: Great, great.

PETER/OWNER: And your meals? They satisfied you?

TED: Absolutely.

PETER/OWNER: Wonderful. Let me know if you need anything else.

TED: Could we see your dessert menu, please?

PETER/OWNER: I'll send my girl right over.

(Smiling at CAROL, PETER/OWNER exits)

CAROL: So. *(Beat)* All the things we've talked about, we never talked about what you do. What do you do, Ted?

TED: I do a lot of different things. You could call me an entrepreneur. Right now I'm in the restaurant business.

CAROL: Oh, you own a restaurant?

TED: I'm a bartender.

CAROL: Oh.

TED: Windows on the World. Top of the Trade Center. I work a day shift tomorrow, come up and I'll buy you a cocktail. You can't go back to Pittsburgh without seeing the city from up there. I'm just doing that for now, in between other things.

CAROL: Don't tell me you're an out of work actor.

TED: Other side of the camera. I went to N Y U for a few semesters, till I realized I don't need a degree to make films. I need money. You know what I'm saying? L O L. I mean, Hahaha.

(MORGAN/WAITRESS enters wearing a burka, hands them both dessert menus, then leaves.)

(CAROL tries to ignore the burka.)

TED: Thank you. So, I am currently raising capital for my next project.

CAROL: Oh, you're making a movie?

TED: A short film.

CAROL: Can I ask what it's about?

TED: Dreams. Or rather fantasies. On the internet.

(MORGAN/WAITRESS *returns with her pad, waits.*)

MORGAN/WAITRESS: According to Joseph Campbell it's not meaning we want in our lives but experience.

TED: You are blushing now.

MORGAN/WAITRESS: We all want to experience rapture…that feeling of being truly alive.

CAROL: Excuse me?

(MORGAN/WAITRESS *pulls off burka.*)

MORGAN/WAITRESS: What can I get you? Pleasure or responsibility.

TED: I'll take the tiramisu.

MORGAN/WAITRESS: *(To* CAROL*)* Addictive isn't it? Like chocolate cake with truffle caramel fudge drizzled all over it. And you can get it with expresso bean ice cream.

CAROL: Uh, no.

MORGAN/WAITRESS: Fine. *(To* TED, *flirty)* Be right back…with dessert.

TED: *(Smiling)* Best part of the meal.

(MORGAN/WAITRESS *exits.* TED *watches her as she walks away. He looks back at* CAROL, *an awkward silence, they smile at each other)*

CAROL: So. You were telling me about your film.

TED: I was telling you about my film. It's all worked out in my head, from start to finish, great visuals. Right now I'm concentrating on getting backing. A national distributor is interested and I told them up front, I want only serious money committed to this project.

CAROL: How much does this have to do with the internet?

TED: The internet was just the inspiration, it's gotten so much bigger than that. That's why I only want serious investors.

(MORGAN/WAITRESS *returns with* TED's *cake. She rolls her eyes at* CAROL *as she exits.*)

CAROL: *(Rubbing her eyes)* Something about her reminds me of my daughter.

TED: *(Looking over his shoulder at retreating waitress)* Oh really? *(Turns his attention to his cake)* Sure you don't want some?

(TED *digs in,* CAROL *watches him consume it.*)

TED: It's really good.

CAROL: How old are you, Ted?

TED: Old enough to rock your world. You're definitely blushing.

CAROL: I'm not blushing. I'm drunk.

TED: But you're here aren't you, and that says something.

(MORGAN/WAITRESS *returns with check, putting it next to* CAROL.)

MORGAN/WAITRESS: Thanks Mom.

CAROL: I beg your pardon.

MORGAN/WAITRESS: I'll take that whenever you're ready.

(But MORGAN/WAITRESS *doesn't leave)*

TED: Here, give that to me. That's mine.

CAROL: Oh that's nice of you, but you don't have to. Thank you.

*(*TED *looks at check and starts patting his pockets.* MORGAN/WAITRESS *looks at* CAROL.*)*

TED: …Uh. This is embarrassing. You know I was so excited to meet you Karen, that I ran out of my apartment without my wallet. I feel like an ass.

CAROL: *(Pulling out her wallet)* Carol.

TED: I'm sorry.

CAROL: My name is Carol, not Karen.

TED: You'll always be Coolbreeze to me.

CAROL: It's not a problem, I was gonna get it anyway. My treat.

*(*CAROL *looks at the bill, tries to cover shock, pulls out credit card.)*

TED: Uhh, you sure you want to pay with a credit card?

CAROL: Oh yeah. Right. Can I give you a check?

MORGAN/WAITRESS: Drivers' license and major credit card.

CAROL: *(Starts writing check)* Can I write it to "cash?"

*(*MORGAN *shrugs,* CAROL *writes)*

CAROL: What's today's date?

MORGAN/WAITRESS: September ninth.

CAROL: *(Writing out a check quickly)* There. *(Hands over her identification)*

MORGAN/WAITRESS: *(Checking license, etc)* Uh huh… *(She exits.)*

TED: *(Tries to take her hand)*

Now you'll have to come back to my apartment so I
can repay you.

CAROL: Oh you don't have to, Ted.

TED: But I want to.

CAROL: I don't think so.

TED: So you really are just a tourist.

CAROL: Are you upset?

TED: You drove across the state of Pennsylvania to buy
me "dinner"?

CAROL: I wanted to meet you.

TED: You wanted to see if we orgasm better together
naked in the same room.

CAROL: I thought we could meet have dinner.

TED: And that's why you stalked me for a week.

CAROL: I wasn't stalking I was sightseeing.

TED: I'm a disappointment to you, aren't I?

CAROL: No, no. *(Beat)* You're young.

TED: I'm not mentioning the fact that you shaved about
a decade off your own age.

CAROL: I wish I could turn back the clock—

TED: If it makes you feel better I can blindfold you.

*(TED pulls out a red blind fold/sleep mask holding it out to
CAROL, an invitation.)*

CAROL: I don't think so…Ted.

TED: I can talk us through the whole thing.

*(CAROL takes it and puts it on. As soon as she is blinded, she
visibly relaxes, giggling.)*

TED: Tall plus dark plus handsome stood up and
helped Coolbreeze to her feet. Her cheeks were flushed
with too much red wine. She fell against him as she

stood, her firm breasts pressing into his chest, for a moment Dark nearly took her down on the floor of the restaurant but the hostile waitress was giving them dirty looks.

(CAROL *laughs, reaching up to pull off the blindfold.* TED *stops her hand.*)

TED: Ted kissed Carol full on the mouth, hard, cutting her lip against her teeth, she tasted blood and knew what she was doing was dangerous, but she felt suddenly free like an animal in the wild, she grabbed his ass and could feel him harden against her belly—

(CAROL *pulls off blindfold, staring at* TED, *tempted*)

TED: You came this far. Now all you got to do is cross over the line.

CAROL: Okay, okay. (*She gets off stool, tripping on her shopping bag with orchid.*) Oh, wait. I almost forgot. I brought this for you.

TED: A plant?

CAROL: An orchid.

TED: Oh yeah, right, right, an orchid. (*He holds up, what is essentially a stem with one blossom left.*)

CAROL: Don't you remember, the first time we talked, you said I reminded you of orchids.

TED: Of course I remember. (*His nose in the blossom, inhales deeply*) I feel like I'm inside you already. Shall we?

(MORGAN/WAITRESS *enters.*)

MORGAN/WAITRESS: The owner wants to talk to you.

CAROL: Oh?

(PETER *as* OWNER *enters.*)

PETER/OWNER: (*Holding out the check*) There's a slight problem. I'm sorry.

CAROL: No, no. I'm sorry. See. He forgot his wallet. And I didn't want to put it on the credit card because… my husband gets the bill…you understand.

PETER/OWNER: We don't accept out of town checks. You understand.

(CAROL *hands credit card to* WAITRESS *who exits.*)

PETER/OWNER: My experience is that they usually don't notice. (*Smiling at* CAROL) Please, come back soon. (*He exits.*)

(WAITRESS *returns.* CAROL *signs the bill, puts card back in her wallet*)

CAROL: Let's go Ted.

(CAROL *exits, red shoes flashing.* TED *follows carrying the orchid like a bag of groceries.*)

(*Fade to black*)

Scene Twelve

(*Sound in the darkness: The last strains of Somewhere Over The Rainbow being played on the saxophone, badly.*)

(*Lights rise on* TED's *studio apartment, which is more hallway than closet. A futon mattress takes up much of the floor, a T V tray with computer and small stool in front of it also doubles as a kitchen table. A dead plant stands near a "window" through which late afternoon sunlight filters in via an airshaft. The orchid in its bag sits next to it. Noise from other similar apartments floats in as the last notes from the saxophone fades.*)

(TED *sits on the edge of the bed as he stops playing his saxophone.* CAROL *stands on the other side of the room [As far as it is possible to go] near the computer and a bottle of tequila*)

TED: High school band. *(Puts down saxophone)* How was that for an aphrodisiac?

CAROL: I'd rather have a drink.

TED: Let's see what we have at the bar.

CAROL: Tequila gone?

TED: Saved you the worm.

CAROL: Maybe some water.

(TED pours her some bottled water into a coffee mug and hands it to CAROL, then eats the worm.)

CAROL: Tell me more about your movie.

TED: It's gonna be shot like a documentary. Black screen. You hear da, da, da, da, da, da, da, dissonant and broken notes, da, da, da, like the twisted dreams of a whole generation. Then you hear this roar and you don't know if it's a train or a tornado, till the camera slowly pulls away and you're barreling along a Miracle Mile, Anywhere, U S A in one of those Monster Tank S U Vs, black and huge. Then suddenly stopping right in front of the camera, it makes a right turn into a vast concrete field, filled with other black monsters. Pull back and we're at the Mall. You're not interested.

CAROL: I am fascinated.

TED: I'll keep going but only if you lie down with me.

CAROL: Okay. *(She awkwardly crawls across futon, lies stiffly next to him, closes her eyes.)* Continue.

TED: *(He takes off her shoes and massages her feet)* Okay, then you see feet, all kinds of feet, walking around, buying stuff, like Materialism. Like that?

CAROL: Mmmm.

TED: At the same time you see people in bed, no not like that, get your mind out of the gutter. Middle aged people in bed asleep. A whole generation in bed asleep, dreaming.

CAROL: What are they dreaming about?

TED: Going to the mall and buying stuff. Get it?

CAROL: What generation are you talking about? Baby boomers?

TED: After that. Old Hippies.

CAROL: The hippies are the baby boomers.

TED: Post hippies, then, the ones that came of age in the seventies.

CAROL: You mean me.

TED: Didn't you come a little later?

CAROL: If you're talking about people in their forties driving S U Vs, going into malls and buying things to take back to their over decorated renovated homes in the suburbs then you are clearly talking about me.

TED: Maybe I am, turn over, on your belly.

(TED *flips* CAROL *over, then climbs on top, massaging her shoulders/back while he continues talking.*)

CAROL: Ohhhkayy…

TED: Okay, we cut from people sleeping to people drinking coffee. Coffee, coffee, coffee, drinking it, pouring it, grinding it, smelling it, cause this film is about the generation—your generation—the generation after the hippies that grew up in the seventies that I call the Zs generation because you can't wake up, caught between dreams— (*His hands wander.*)

CAROL: Watch it buddy.

TED: Caught between the "love the world" fantasy of the sixties and the "love the money" fantasy of the eighties. You are unable to wake yourselves up, but you lean toward the money, of course. Then came the

90s and the bombing of little brown people we don't like so we can continue to gas up those S U Vs and drive to the mall.

CAROL: For someone who's never owned a car you seem particularly obsessed by them.

TED: Present day: September 2001, we're coming to the end of the first year of the new millenium, but as long as you can drive to Starbucks for your double mocha decaf latte it doesn't matter who has to die for the gas to get you there.

CAROL: All this love talk is too much for me, Ted.

TED: But now there is the Internet, which is One Big Dream. Cut to all these staring faces, clicking away trying to connect with whatever. Doesn't matter. It's about the act. No faces, just imagination. This is where I'll have the live video cam of women having sex with barnyard animals.

CAROL: *(Rolling over to face him)* Whaaaat?

TED: Just checkin your hearin. No, but I will have a web porn collage thing here, for visuals, to show what people are really doing and why. Like us.

CAROL: It's about us?

TED: It's about America. Sexual Imagination. And the Internet.

CAROL: So I'm research?

TED: Are you gonna kiss me yet?

CAROL: I'm afraid to Ted.

TED: You're going to prove my theory.

CAROL: What theory is that?

TED: That people today aren't interested in having actual sex, except of course as a necessary bodily function, no, they much prefer the clean mind blowing sex of their imaginations.

CAROL: I like real sex, Ted.

TED: Really?

CAROL: Really.

TED: Then blow me.

CAROL: It's not that simple.

TED: It is actually very simple. See online you'd blow me in a millisecond. Because it's easy, it's clean, it's sweat free, and it doesn't smell; there are no surprises, because it all happens on the screen, which, and this is the point of my film, the screen really acts like a mirror. We see exactly what we project onto it, and who we really want to have sex with is ourselves.

CAROL: That's not true, I much prefer another person helping out. What I mean is, in bed, with you, I can't just type it in, I need to feel it and to feel it I need a little atmosphere. *(She attempts to get off the bed)* Blow me. Maybe that's hip, I call it crude. I know you can do better.

TED: *(Pulling her back on top of him)* You're right. I was just making a point. About my film.

CAROL: I don't like your film.

TED: Forget the film. Are you attracted to me?

CAROL: Since I am piss drunk and have no judgement, the answer is yes. The idea of you is very sexy; the fact of you brings up all sorts of uncomfortable things, which I can't seem to make myself forget, no matter how many bad drink choices I continue to make, like the fact that I have a family.

TED: In Pittsburgh.

CAROL: Also I still don't like your film.

TED: Forget the film. That was just filler. Close your eyes and pretend you're on the internet, and you're dreaming this. (*Pulls red blind fold from his pocket*) Want me to blind fold you?

CAROL: No. If I close my eyes I'll start snoring.

TED: Wouldn't bother me.

(TED *kisses* CAROL *with her eyes wide open staring at him. He becomes more passionate. She keeps staring. He drapes her arms around him and begins pawing at her very unromantically. She closes her eyes and tries to join in.*)

(*But they bump heads, then teeth, elbows and knees get in the way. He tries to get her dress off smoothly, but finally she has to stop and work it off herself. He tries to get her slip off in the same suave way, but she has to stop and help him there too. She tries to get his clothes off, he stops and does it himself. They roll off the futon, climb back on, he is clumsy, but persistent. Finally she sits up half dressed in an impossibly awkward position, pushes him off her*)

CAROL: Stop.

(TED *tries to kiss* CAROL *again.*)

CAROL: This isn't working.

TED: Want me to talk during it?

CAROL: NO! I want you to stop, Ted.

TED: Why? Examine it. Go ahead.

CAROL: Because the whole point of this, right from the beginning, was so I could *lose* myself. To make *Carol,* boring, middle aged, soul-less Carol, disappear, but instead every time you kiss me, I get bigger and bigger in this impossible to hide in little room and there is no avoiding the fact that I am an asshole.

TED: No you're not.

CAROL: Okay, then you are. *(Putting on her clothes)* I feel like a cliché.

TED: Thank you. That's what I tell all those wannabe critics of my work. It's cliché. Right, well people feel like cliches everyday.

CAROL: I gotta call Peter. I gotta talk to Peter.

TED: *(Lies back, spread-eagled on futon, hands over head)* I guess this means you're not going to invest in my film.

CAROL: What in the world was I thinking?

TED: Hold on a minute and I can tell you. *(He pulls out a folder from a cardboard box under the computer table, looks through it, finds one.)* ...Here: *(Reading)* "We are standing on a rooftop. It is dark, but there is enough moonlight to see the desire in each other's eyes. I let you unbutton my blouse. You touch my bare breast, I breathe in sharply, from pleasure so intense it feels like pain. Your mouth comes down wet and soft on my nipple which immediately—"

CAROL: You kept a file on me?

TED: You got better as you went along: "My uterus exploded in ecstasy and you didn't even touch me, I only thought about you as I fingered the keys and I came in a rock hard explosion—"

CAROL: I never wrote that.

TED: *(Checking the paper)* Oh. No, you didn't. *(He looks through the other folders.)* They're all mixed up.

CAROL: How many women did you do this too?

TED: Hey, not to, with. The internet is a two way street.

CAROL: *(Pulling on the rest of her clothes)* I should've known.

TED: I like talking to women. Is there something wrong with that? Women have a lot to say; I find them so interesting. Whenever a man, you know, is pretending he's a woman, I can always tell by the lack of originality— *(Pause)* What?

CAROL: I thought. We were so intimate together, I assumed—

TED: Exclusivity?

CAROL: That it meant something to you.

TED: Of course it meant something. I saved yours. You were someone I always looked forward to. You have a way with words. In fact you're writing got better as we went along. Ever think about writing screenplays?

CAROL: Oh god. I gotta go.

TED: Before you go. Would you mind signing this release form? I think this is great stuff, really, and I want to put it in the film. I don't think you're cliché—at least not in a bad way.

(CAROL grabs her "file" and stuffs it into the shopping bag with the orchid.)

CAROL: I'm taking this with me.

TED: Don't drive back tonight. You can stay here. I won't bother you. I'll be online anyway. You can have the futon.

CAROL: I've got a hotel. Thank you. *(She looks at him a moment.)* Water your plant, Ted.

(CAROL exits. TED looks at the plant for a moment, then back to his files. As he rearranges them alphabetically)

TED: I tried to tell you… *(He stuffs them back in the box and shoves the box back under the computer. He sits in front of the computer, snaps it on, sighs. He shakes out his hands a little, then signs on.)*

(Lights lower and reflect the computer glow on TED's face, staring at the screen. Sound of the keys, clacking)

Scene Thirteen

TED: I'm dreaming that I'm walking through a blizzard. There are white outs and snow drifts flying past while I blast ahead. It's a wild ride, my feet barely skimming the ground. On the sidelines, in my peripheral vision are all the women I've ever talked to: starting with my mother and my sisters and the girl I had a crush on in sixth grade and Lorrie from college and the women in my building and all those ladies on the internet. It makes a beautiful montage, and I'm thinking to myself, cause I know it's a dream: Remember this when you wake up! Then just as I'm thinking this, something slaps me in the face. It's a piece of paper. And that's when I realize I'm in a paper storm, surrounded by flying pieces of paper, which I figure out are all the emails I ever sent in my life. And as I am picking up speed, moving faster and faster I'm trying to read what is on all the paper, and then I realize I couldn't stop even if I wanted to, so I think to myself enjoy the ride. And then I'm moving down a long wind tunnel filled with paper whipping past, I'm shooting like an arrow smack into the world wide web! This is the internet, man! I'm actually in the internet! I start taking it all in, all of it. I let go of every day reality, and keep falling and falling. There's no bottom. (*Beat*) And I never wake up.

(*Lights shift back to Pittsburgh*)

Scene Fourteen

(*Pittsburgh. September 10, 2001. Evening*)

(PETER *sits in the middle of the great room, eating a sandwich.* CAROL *walks in. They look at each other across* "the grand canyon." *Silence.* PETER *continues eating his sandwich.*)

CAROL: I'm back.

PETER: I see that.

CAROL: Why are you sitting in the dark?

PETER: The power went out.

CAROL: Did the kitchen blow another fuse?

PETER: No it's not the kitchen. The whole block is out, if you didn't notice. We're all sitting in the dark.

CAROL: No, I didn't notice. It's dusk.

PETER: In between light and dark. Can't trust what you see now.

CAROL: I didn't go to Florida. I went to New York. Peter, I violated the integrity of our marriage. I didn't actually go through with it, there was no— what's the word—

PETER: *(Overlapping)* Penetration?

CAROL: No. It's a different word.

PETER: Fornication.

CAROL: No.

PETER: Adultery.

CAROL: No. Consummation, that's the word I wanted.

PETER: So you didn't consummate your affair with a stranger you met on the internet.

CAROL: Morgan told you?

PETER: Of course she told me, and it wasn't fair to put her in that position. She had a rough time this week; she thought you were dead.

CAROL: Where is she?

PETER: She's upstairs doing her homework.

CAROL: In the dark?

PETER: She has a lot of homework.

CAROL: You have every right to be mad at me, to hate me, but I am sorry. I lost my way I think I lost my way, somehow.

PETER: It seems to me, you lost your mind.

CAROL: *(Starting to cry)* That too.

PETER: Don't cry for my sake, please.

CAROL: *(Pulls orchid out of the bag, just a stem)* I thought you couldn't kill these plants. Someone told me they live on anything, pulling what they need out of the air. Actually they are horribly easy to kill.

PETER: That's not dead.

CAROL: It's not?

PETER: They lose their blossoms. They grow back, but you have to take care of it, give it what it needs. Humidity mostly. You could even clone another one from that one. It takes patience though.

CAROL: How do you know this?

PETER: I know about orchids. I don't know why, picked it up somewhere, more useless information.

CAROL: I didn't know you knew about orchids.

PETER: There's a lot you don't know.

CAROL: It was just fantasizing Peter, late at night when everybody else was asleep. I never meant it to go this far.

PETER: But you got in the car and you drove to New York and you stayed there a week.

CAROL: I did.

PETER: I can hear the dinner conversations now. "Did you hear what happened to Peter and Carol?" "No, what?" "Carol ran away with a man she met on the internet." "Poor Peter." Sucker.

CAROL: I wanted to do something that would wake me up and having sex with a stranger seemed like it would do it. The first time he saw me naked, the first time he kissed me, it didn't happen like that, but I thought it would be an experience, that would make me feel something before the rest of my life, became a slow, mudslide into Aunt Tessiehood. I don't want to be my Aunt Tessie.

PETER: We all get old.

CAROL: It's different for you; it's different for men.

PETER: I have had one dream since the day I realized I loved you and that day didn't come easy. I resisted you that whole first year. I wished that I'd met you later, a few more years down the road. There was so much more I wanted to do before a wife and baby. You were beautiful and funny, but also neurotic and needy and way too emotional and I realized in that moment I fell in love with you that I would never scale mountains or live on a houseboat in the Carribbean or hitchhike to Peru. I would take that job in accounting, buy a fixer upper, have a family and grow old with you. And I didn't want anything else except to still be holding your hand when I was eighty.

(Beat)

CAROL: I'll go to Peru with you.

PETER: No. I don't need to go anywhere anymore. Because all this time I thought I was going somewhere—with you. (Beat) So, maybe I lost my way too.

CAROL: Can you...still love me?

PETER: Fool that I am.

CAROL: So...do you...forgive me?

PETER: There's no quick fix. You broke something between us. It's broke. You can't just delete it and start over. It's like the roof. We've got to call a roofer and decide, are we gonna do a patch job or tear the whole thing down for something new.

CAROL: *(Moving toward him)* I'm willing to do either.

PETER: *(Stopping her)* If you touch me now, I'm going to get angry and I don't want to do that, so...

(MORGAN enters with a flashlight.)

MORGAN: Mom? Are you okay? I'm sorry. I told Daddy.

CAROL: I know, it's all right.

MORGAN: Are you guys getting divorced?

(Brief pause)

CAROL & PETER: *(Speaking at the same time)* No.

CAROL: Daddy tells me you've had a lot of work this week.

MORGAN: Yeah.

CAROL: You know Morgan I was thinking I should know more about what you're doing. You know the letter writing and the other stuff, I should come with you, on one of your protests or we could go to a soup kitchen together.

MORGAN: You don't have to, Mom.

CAROL: Send me all the emails you want, I'll read every one.

MORGAN: I wrote my essay. Actually I rewrote it. Want to hear it?

CAROL: Yes.

MORGAN: *(Pulls out crumpled up paper)* Don't panic. This is just my draft. *(Reads)* To Whom It May Concern.

While attempting to write this essay I have come to realize the impossibility of explaining myself to a group of strangers who will make a decision about me that will change my life forever. Since I am giving you the awesome responsibility to alter my destiny, by opening or closing the door that could lead me toward or away from the person I was meant to be, I have a right to know who you are, beyond the course catalogue and college brochures. As the customer in this exchange, after all, I ask you to respond in essay form to my seven questions: *(Still reading but slower, directing it to* CAROL*)*

Number One: how are you going to help me reach my destiny? Two: Keep my dreams alive? Three: Teach me to appreciate the now? Four: Live in harmony with the earth? Five: Love my fellow human? Six: Pass on what I've learned to the next generation and Seven: prepare my soul to die? *(Beat)* Organize your answers in a carefully thought out and well-written essay. You can be sure that your essay will be critical in my decision making process. *(Beat)* What do you think? Daddy helped, a little.

CAROL: *(Softly sarcastic)* I think that will get you into a lot of schools.

MORGAN: Just the ones I want.

CAROL: *(Beat)* How'd you grow up so fast?

*(*MORGAN *shines flashlight onto orchid.)*

MORGAN: You know what Dorothy finally says. If you don't find it in your own backyard, you never really lost it. *(She picks up the orchid and places it on the kitchen island.)*

CAROL: I never understood that.

MORGAN: It makes sense if you turn it around. You can't find what you didn't lose.

CAROL: I'm sorry Morgan.

MORGAN: No, I'm sorry. You're a good Mom. I'd be lucky to be like you.

CAROL: Commere, honey. *(She embraces* MORGAN, *whispering fiercely.)* Hold onto yourself Morgan, that's what you should do.

MORGAN: Okay. *(Hugging her back)* I'm glad you're home. *(Beat)* Well, it's dark. I think I'll leave you two alone. 'Nite. *(She exits.)*

CAROL: Coolbreeze took a step toward Regular guy 8762

PETER: Regular guy, that's me. Along with 8,761 other guys.

CAROL: She reached out a hand to touch his face.

PETER: Don't.

CAROL: It felt like a century since she touched this face. It was rough and stubbly, graying but warm and full of character and his eyes always brightened a little when he looked at her, and she never failed to notice this, even when it seemed she was not paying attention. It was comfort, this face. She could curl up in it and fall asleep there, feeling safe forever.

PETER: Like an old easy chair left on the curb for the garbage pickers.

(CAROL pauses. Tries again)

CAROL: Driving home, when I was about an hour away, you know that last stretch through the mountains? I pulled over in Somerset. I was terrified to walk into this house and face you. So I was buying some time. I parked at the side of the road, looking across a wide open field. It had been a beautiful heart crunching blue sky day, and now that the sun was going down, the sky was pink and gold and I thought

I have absolutely no right to be this unhappy. I've been taking you for granted like everything else in my life. And I don't want to do that anymore.

(Beat)

PETER: I'll call the roofer tomorrow.

CAROL: Are you going to bed?

PETER: Tomorrow's going to be a full day.

CAROL: Okay. I might stay up a little while. Wind down. Check, check my email. Just my email. I mean I'm just going to delete my entire account and start over.

PETER: Okay. Good night. *(He exits.)*

CAROL: 'Night.

(As CAROL opens her laptop and starts it up lights rise on a SHADOWY FIGURE behind her.)

(PETER re-enters, and holds out his hand to CAROL)

PETER: There's time to start over tomorrow. Come to bed.

(CAROL hesitates, the internet glowing behind her. She shuts the laptop.)

(The SHADOWY FIGURE fades as PETER and CAROL face each other.)

(CAROL reaches out to take PETER's hand. The buzzing from the computer grows into a faint roar, under CAROL's final speech.)

SCENE SIXTEEN

(CAROL, *alone*)

CAROL: I dream I am at the edge of a dark forest with my Brain, my Heart and my Courage, standing at the place where three rivers merge. Out of this, a fourth underground river flows, and out of that a clear voice asks me if I am a good witch or a bad witch. I look down and see I am wearing red shoes. I ask my Brain, which way? He answers, "Who are you?" I kiss him goodbye first and tell him, I will miss him most of all. Then I put my heart in my pocket, and, wearing my courage like a coat, decide it's time to find my way back to Kansas. I pay no attention to the man behind the curtain and with my red shoes discover I can walk on the water. I am laughing. And crying. Because the tornado is coming. Good or bad, I know that nothing will ever be the same again.

(*The roar of the tornado grows.*)

(*Blackout*)

END OF PLAY